NUREG/IA-0405

I0413167

International Agreement Report

Coupling the RELAP Code with External Calculation Programs (Shared Memory Version)

Prepared by:
Felix Maciel

Comisión Nacional de Energía Atómica
Centro Atómico Bariloche
San Carlos de Bariloche
R8402AGP, Argentina

A. Calvo, NRC Project Manager

Office of Nuclear Regulatory Research
U.S. Nuclear Regulatory Commission
Washington, DC 20555-0001

Manuscript Completed: September 2011
Date Published: October 2011

Prepared as part of
The Agreement on Research Participation and Technical Exchange
Under the Thermal-Hydraulic Code Applications and Maintenance Program (CAMP)

Published by
U.S. Nuclear Regulatory Commission

International Agreement Report

Coupling the RELAP Code with External Calculation Programs (Shared Memory Version)

Prepared by:
Felix Maciel

Comisión Nacional de Energía Atómica
Centro Atómico Bariloche
San Carlos de Bariloche
R8402AGP, Argentina

A. Calvo, NRC Project Manager

Office of Nuclear Regulatory Research
U.S. Nuclear Regulatory Commission
Washington, DC 20555-0001

Manuscript Completed: September 2011
Date Published: October 2011

Prepared as part of
The Agreement on Research Participation and Technical Exchange
Under the Thermal-Hydraulic Code Applications and Maintenance Program (CAMP)

Published by
U.S. Nuclear Regulatory Commission

ABSTRACT

A communication library has been developed for the connection of external calculation programs to the RELAP code using shared memory techniques. Modifications to the RELAP program have been introduced in order to implement these facilities.

A portable (non multi-platform) version of the communication library has been achieved, producing a reliable, good performance coupling.

This permits exporting variables from RELAP, operating with them in an external program, and transferring them back to RELAP, working in a synchronized way.

CONTENTS

Figures

1. INTRODUCTION

In the frame of the thermal hydraulic analysis required for supporting the Probabilistic Safety Analysis (Level 1) of Atucha II NPP, several transient and accident scenarios have been simulated with RELAP5/MOD3.3 patch 3 1.

For the simulation of the Reactor Protection system, Limitation system, Control system and interlocking, as well as the reactivity evaluation, it was necessary to couple an external calculation FORTRAN program to RELAP 2 3. The reason was the limitation found in the normal resources available in RELAP, mainly related to the maximum number of control variables that can be used to simulate the complex systems above mentioned. The previous experience modelling Atucha I NPP confirmed the necessity of implementing this alternative.

The external calculation program used for this particular purpose was based on the DYNETZ code 4. However, the procedure enables the coupling of any external program.

A communication library has been developed for the connection between the external programs and the RELAP code using shared memory techniques. Modifications to the original RELAP program have been introduced in order to implement these facilities.

This permits exporting variables from RELAP, operating with them in an external program, and transferring them back to RELAP, working in a synchronized way.

The programming of the internal and external modules required for the programs coupling is outlined in the following sections.

2. PROGRAMMING OF THE RELAP CODE INTERNAL MODULE

2.1 General description

The internal module is composed by a set of FORTRAN subroutines that makes use of the shared memory calls of the Win32 system to establish a communication channel between the RELAP code and the external calculation program. All the extra code has been included in the source files *iconvr.ff* and *convar.ff*; additionally, the header files *cnvtpa.hh* and *cnvtpad.hh* and the source files *dtstep.ff*, *rconvr.ff* and *tran.ff* have been modified.

This set of subroutines and modifications to the RELAP code **should not be changed** as it has been specially developed to be activated in the 'communication with external programs' mode, as it is described below, in case that variables of the type **ovar** or **ivar** are declared in the configuration and modeling files of the RELAP code; this automatically activates the communication with an external program in case that the RELAP code has been compiled with this option.

In case that the RELAP code has not been compiled for the communication with external programs, an error message will be produced during the initialization process as the variables **ovar** and/or **ivar** will not be recognized.

2.2 Control components added to RELAP

Two new components have been implemented in the context of the control system (cards 205CCC00 or 205CCCC0): **ivar** (input variable, based on RELAP control variable **constant**) and **ovar** (output variable, based on RELAP control variable **poweri**).

2.2.1 Component IVAR

In the components of the type **ivar** the third word of the card 205CCC00 (or 205CCCC0) W3(R) **will not** be a scaling factor but it will correspond to the initial value of this variable. For this type of component, the rest of the cards 205CCC01-CCC09 or 205CCCC1-CCCC9 must not be entered.

2.2.2 Component OVAR

The components of the type **ovar** are defined as:

$$Y = S V_1$$

W1(A)   Alphanumeric name of the variable request code for V_1
W2(I)   Integer name of the variable request code for V_1
W3(I)   1 (one) or 0 (zero) (Currently not used, it can be used for outputs activation/deactivation)

S and the limits are defined in the component type card.

2.3 Communication with the external program

The communication with the external program is established by means of subroutines programmed in the source files *iconvr.ff* and *convar.ff*. These subroutines allocate the variables for the communication with RELAP in the COMMON *ctrldata*. **The COMMON must contain REAL type variables in order to be managed by the RELAP pre-processor.**

The limit for the number of variables that the arrays *Entradas* and *Salidas* can contain is defined through the parameter *grande* (currently 1023). This value **should be** modified very carefully as it is related to the variable *transfer* which controls the low level communication.

2.4 Internal states

The internal states and the shared memory communication system data, together with multiple access protections, are stored in the COMMON *memdata*; they are the reference to the shared memory and several flags that the operative system uses as event managers.

2.5 Communication programming

2.5.1 Communication initialization

The communication initialization process is performed by a three stage exchange to establish the data channel between the RELAP code and the external program.

If, during the initialization of the RELAP code run, the declaration of a variable of the type **ivar** and/or **ovar** is found in the configuration and/or modeling files (processing achieved in the source file *iconvr.ff*) the subroutine *iodataini* is called, and if the variable is of the **ovar** type the subroutine *mando* is called for the variable initialization in the communication with the external program.

The first time the subroutine *iodataini* is called, this in turn calls the subroutine *inicmem* to initialize the shared memory subsystem and create also a communication pipe and wait for the contact with the external program, with a maximum waiting time of 600 seconds; if no contact is established within that time, the subroutine terminates the RELAP run with an error message.

Once the connection is produced, connection parameters as well as the configuration file name and the restart number of the current run are exchanged. After this, the connection is properly established and initialized.

Following, the subroutine *iodata* is invoked to produce the first data transfer to the external program for the initialization of its variables.

2.5.2 Communication at each time step

The subroutine *convar* calls the subroutine *mando* at each time step for every variable of the types **ivar** and/or **ovar** in order to copy the datum into the communication structures of the shared memory; after this loop process, the subroutine *iodata* is invoked to perform the actual communication by means of the shared memory copy system, and then the control variables processing loop is initiated, where the variables **ivar** are extracted from the communication structure by the subroutine *recibo*.

2.5.3   Communication finalization

During the execution of the last time step of the RELAP code run, the end of the calculation is detected in the subroutine *tran* (source file *tran.ff*) and the closure call to the subroutine *iodata* is made, with the flag set to -1, meaning that this is the last message, carrying no useful data.

After this, the RELAP code run terminates, neither waiting any response from the external program nor producing an explicit closure of the shared memory system.

3. PROGRAMMING OF THE EXTERNAL MODULE

3.1 General description

The external module is a FORTRAN program that utilizes the shared memory calls of the Win32 system for the communication with the RELAP code. The source files associated to this program are *CtrlExterno.f*, *CtrlExt_Lib.f*, *inic.f*, *paso.f* and *term.f*; that require the header files *CtrlExt.h* and *CtrlExt_Lib.h*. These in turn obtain information from the header files *grande_size.h* and *ctrldata.h*.

The source file *CtrlExterno.f* contains the main program. The source file *CtrlExt_Lib.f* contains all the subroutines for the communication with RELAP by means of the shared memory calls of the Win32 system, including the process of reading and writing of a binary data storing file (called *xxxx_REG.res*, where *xxxx* is the file name identifying the RELAP simulation run). This file stores all the data necessary for the external control algorithm to initiate a simulation from a "restart" point.

Neither these two source files (*CtrlExterno.f* and *CtrlExt_Lib.f*) nor the header file (*CtrlExt_Lib.h*) need to be modified by the control algorithm programmer, and it is recommended not to do so.

The control algorithm must be programmed in the source files *inic.f*, *paso.f* and *term.f*. All the calculations required for the algorithm initialization must be performed in the file *inic.f*; a time step for this algorithm must be defined in the file *paso.f*; and all the calculations required for the algorithm finalization, if necessary, must be made in the file *term.f*.

3.2 Communication with RELAP

The communication with the RELAP code is performed through the subroutines programmed in the source file *CtrlExt_Lib.f*. These subroutines allocate the variables for the communication with RELAP in the COMMON statements *Entradas*, *BaseTiempo* and *Salidas*. **All these COMMONs must contain variables of the type REAL *8.**

For each calculation interval, two variables are updated in the COMMON *BaseTiempo*: the first one, *Time* (the RELAP simulation time), and the second one, *DTime* (the RELAP time step). The programmer can change the name of these variables, taking into account the described sequential order, and the requirement that the variables must be defined as REAL*8.

For each calculation interval also, all the variables that RELAP transfer to the control program are updated in the COMMON *Entradas*. The user can choose convenient names for these variables (that must be of the type REAL *8), considering that their sequential order must be coincident with the order in which RELAP transfers them to the control program.

The user transfers to the RELAP code the result of all the control actions for each time step through the COMMON *Salidas*. RELAP receives them in the same order as they are listed in this COMMON. Also these variables must be of the type REAL *8.

The limit for the number of variables contained in the COMMONs *Entradas* and *Salidas* is controlled by the parameter *grande* included in the file *grande_size.h*.

3.3   Internal states

In the definition of the control algorithm it is often necessary to store a set of variables from a time interval for the following one. These variables are referred to as internal states and they must be stored in the corresponding "restart" file in order to be recalled for a "restart" calculation. The user can list these REAL *8 type variables in COMMONs. The file *Restart_commons.h* contains the COMMONs definition and the files *Read_restart.h* and *Write_Restart.h* contain the corresponding read/write codes.

3.4   Algorithm programming

In this section, the procedure for the control algorithm programming inside the external control program is presented. A general flow chart of the program is showed in Fig.1. In the following sub sections, the algorithm initialization, the calculation at each time interval and the algorithm finalization are described, specifying the source files where these processes are to be performed.

3.4.1   Algorithm initialization

The control algorithm initialization must be programmed in the source file *inic.f*, in the subroutine *inicializacion*, which is called by the main program just once at the beginning of the program execution (see Fig.1). The subroutine *inicializacion* calls first the subroutine *InicCom*, which initializes the communication with RELAP and performs the first communication operations.

In this early stage, *InicCom* receives the file name identifying the simulation run and an integer variable indicating whether the calculation starts at time equal zero (the variable value is 0 in this case) or it is initiated from a "restart" point (the integer variable value means the iteration number where the new simulation starts).

The subroutine *InicCom* returns an integer value indicating whether the initiated simulation run starts at time equal zero (the variable value is 0) or from a "restart" point (the variable value is 1).

The control algorithm initialization is mainly intended for the case of starting a simulation run from time equal zero, rather than for a "restart" run, as it is showed in Fig.1, in which after calling the subroutine *InicCom*, the value of the return integer variable is analyzed and if it is 0 (simulation starts at time equal zero) the initialization *calculations* are performed. Once the IF execution ends, the execution of the subroutine *inicializacion* finalizes returning the control to the main program.

NOTE: For the initialization process, the initial conditions for all the integrators included in the control algorithm must be adequately set (corresponding to an internal state variable or an input/output variable). A proper initialization relies upon the responsibility of the user programming the external control algorithm.

3.4.2 Calculation at each time interval

In the control algorithm, the calculation at each time interval must be programmed in the source file *paso.f*, in the subroutine *paso* which is called at each calculation step by the main program. This subroutine must return an integer number indicating whether the simulation is terminated or not; if so, the main program terminates the calculation loop and calls the subroutine for the simulation run finalization. This integer number must be 0 for continuing with the calculation, and a non-zero value for the algorithm finalization.

First, the subroutine *paso* calls the subroutine *LeeCom* to read all the variables that RELAP transfers to the external control program at a time step (see Fig.1). The subroutine *LeeCom* also stores -at intervals controlled by RELAP- all the variables in the COMMONs *Entradas*, *BaseTiempo*, *Estados* and *Salidas*, necessary for an eventual restart run.

The subroutine *LeeCom* returns an integer variable indicating whether the calculation loop must terminate (its value is 1) or it must continue (the value is 0). If the returning value is 1, the subroutine *paso* returns the control to the main program, setting the variable *NFLAG* to 1, to make the main program exit the calculation loop. Otherwise, the subroutine *paso* performs the control algorithm calculation.

Once the algorithm calculation is achieved, the internal state variables must be updated for the next time step, and after that the subroutine *EscCom* is called to transfer to RELAP all the variables in the COMMON *Salidas* calculated in the control algorithm (if any of these variables is not updated, the value calculated in the previous time step will be transferred).

After calling *EscCom*, the subroutine returns the control to the main program.

NOTE: The program does not update the internal state variables, therefore the programming user must implement the updating process where described in this section.

3.4.3 Algorithm finalization

Once the simulation execution terminates, the main program calls (externally to the calculation loop) the subroutine *terminacion* programmed in the source file *term.f* (see Fig.1). At this point, the calculations for the finalization of the control algorithm execution must be performed, if necessary (usually not necessary).

When these calculations are achieved, the subroutine calls *FinCom* prior to return the control to the main program. The subroutine *FinCom* stores the data corresponding to the COMMONs *Entradas*, *BaseTiempo*, *Estados* and *Salidas* for an eventual restart run from this last calculated time. After this, *FinCom* closes properly the communication with RELAP.

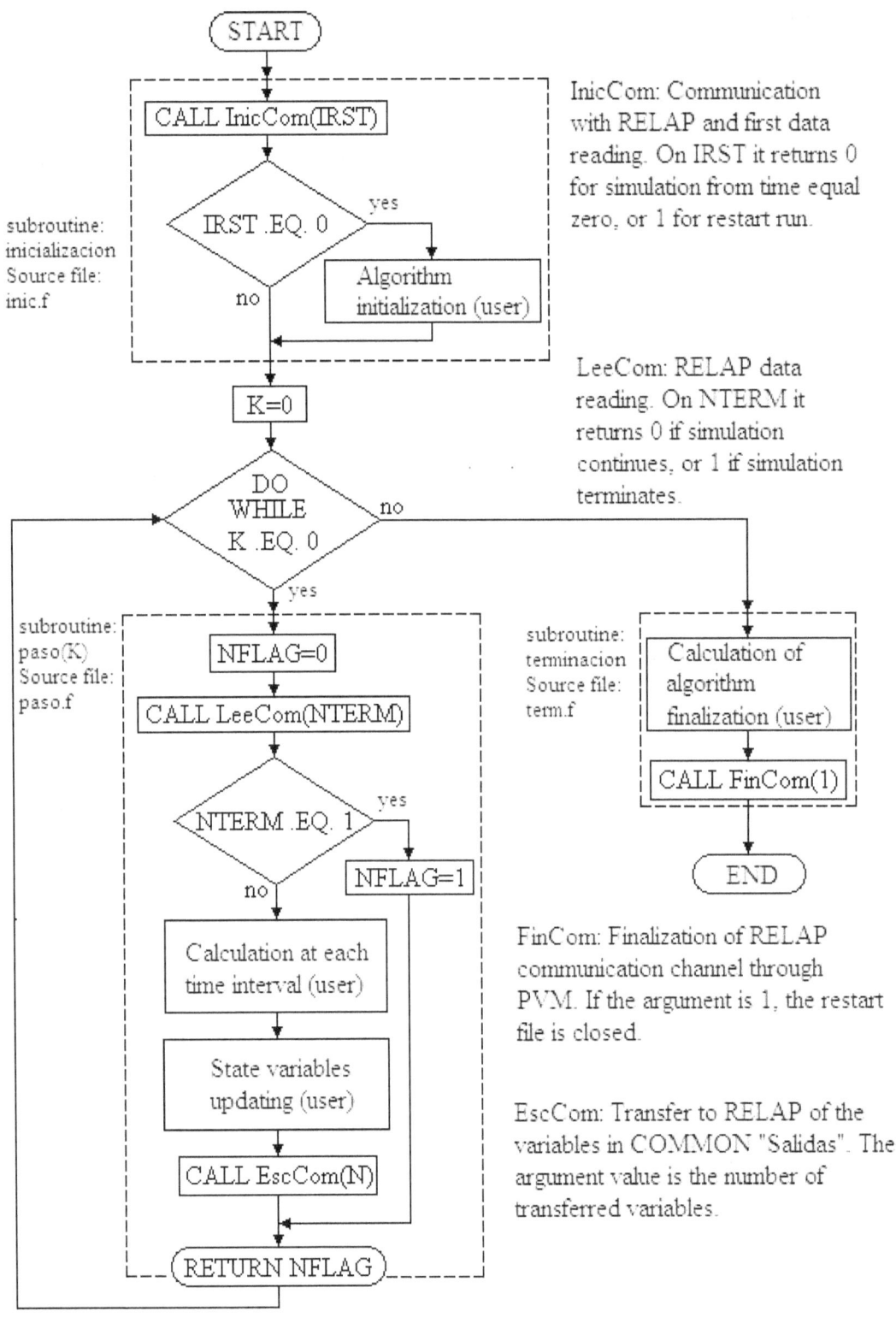

Fig. 1 -. Flow chart of the external control program.

4. CONCLUSIONS

A communication library has been developed for the connection of external calculation programs to the RELAP code using shared memory techniques. Modifications to the RELAP program have been introduced in order to implement these facilities.

This permits exporting variables from RELAP, operating with them in an external program, and transferring them back to RELAP, working in a synchronized way.

The programming of the internal and external modules required for the programs coupling has been outlined. The result is a portable (non multi-platform) version of the communication library, producing a reliable, good performance coupling.

5. REFERENCES

1. Information Systems Laboratories, Inc., *RELAP5/MOD3.3 Code Manual*, Vol. 1 to 7, January 2002

2. Maciel, F, *Coupling the RELAP code to FORTRAN programs*, Technical Report under preparation.

3. Schivo, M. A., *CtrlExterno - Descripción del programa de simulación de las lógicas de control de la CNA II para la nodalización con RELAP*, Technical Report NA-SA TN/777/2006, Lima, Bs. As., October 2006.

4. Hirmer, F., *CNA2: Beschreibung des Arbeitsablaufes zur Durchführung von Transientenanalysen mit dem Programm DYNETZ auf dem Personalcomputer (PC) unter MS-DOS*, Technical Report KWU NDS1/99/2067, Erlangen, May 1999.

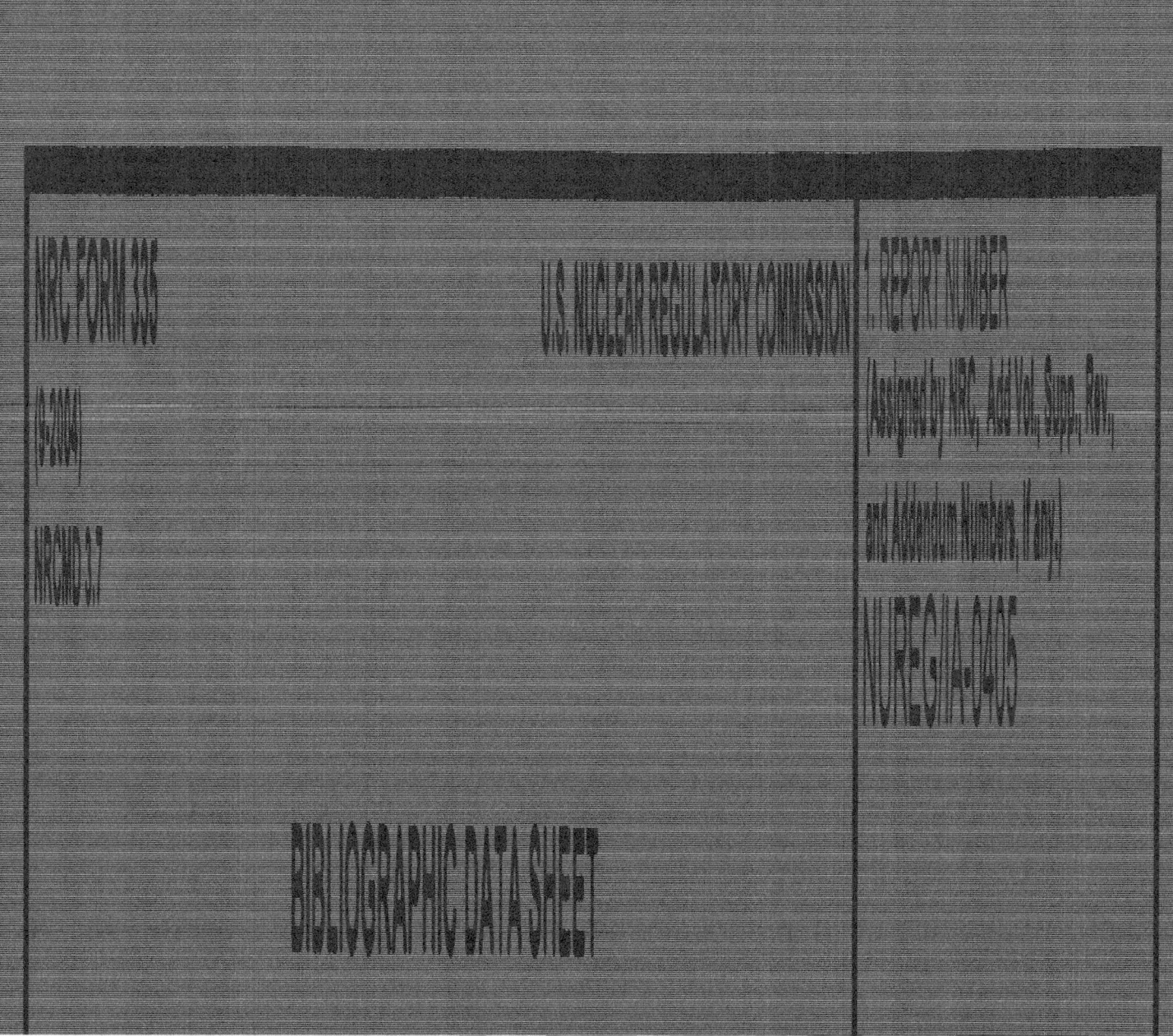

NRC FORM 335
(9-2004)
NRCMD 3.7

U.S. NUCLEAR REGULATORY COMMISSION

1. REPORT NUMBER
(Assigned by NRC, Add Vol., Supp., Rev.,
and Addendum Numbers, if any.)

NUREG/IA-0405

BIBLIOGRAPHIC DATA SHEET

Printed
on recycled
paper

Federal Recycling Program

UNITED STATES
NUCLEAR REGULATORY COMMISSION
WASHINGTON, DC 20555-0001

OFFICIAL BUSINESS

NUREG/IA-0405

Coupling the RELAP Code with External Calculation Programs
(Shared Memory Version)

October 2011